Also by Freda Chaney

~Prose~

7 Days: Manifesting the Life You Want

http://www.7daysmanifestingthelifeyouwant.com

Karma Road: Walking through Time with George Eliot

http://www.karmaroadwalkingthroughtime.com

~Poetry~

http://www.puttingby.com

Oh god, Papa

Poems

Freda M. Chaney

Copyright © 2015

Freda M. Chaney

All rights reserved.

Printed in the U.S.A.

First Edition, September 7, 2015

Book cover and interior design by Freda M. Chaney

ISBN-10: 1517238560
ISBN-13: 978-1517238568

For my mother, Lois, who passed too soon,
but left her music in my heart.

∞

Contents

Poems

Marking Time	1
Knowing	3
Putting By	4
Woodland Bird (for Gerard Manley Hopkins)	6
Apple Towns (for Dylan Thomas)	7
Things That Stay	9
Holding Fast	10
Papa	11
Sugar Creek (for the Amish)	13
Enough	14
Bloomingdale	15
Promise Like Stone	16
The Offering	18
Seeing Red	19
Potatoes	20
Broken Wing (for George Eliot)	22
Layers of Meaning	23
Old Joe (for John Steinbeck)	24

The Girl Who Peed Her Pants	26
Loosening (for Walt Whitman)	28
No One's Princess	29
Game Show Salvation	30
A Well	31
Willows	32
The Gathering at Emerson's (for Ralph Waldo Emerson	33
Harmony	35
Universal Rhythm	36
Apocalypse	37
On 66 Heading West (for Jack Kerouac)	39
Talking	41
Soul Brown	42
Mother	43
Nature Within (for Thomas Merton)	44
Etude in White (for Emily Dickinson)	47
Becoming	48
Faith	49
Ignored	50
Colors of America (for U.S. patriots)	51
Never!	52
Sirens	53

And So We Write	54
Armies of Salvation	55
Linoleum	56
Half-Light	57
Passage	60
A Gordon	61
Valeur du Temps	62
When? (for D.H. Lawrence)	63
Somewhere Down the Road	64
All Lucy-like in Narnia (for C.S. Lewis)	65
The Color of Pain	66
Man is a Farmer	67
Indestructible	68
Not So Solitary	70
Who Yer Mama?	71
Libre Spiritus	72
The Yellow Piano	74
Steel Town Blues (for Steubenville)	76
Faux Pas	77
Celtic K(not)	78
The Pizza Shop Lady	79
When Fall Apples Fall	82

Teddy Bear and Mr. Clown (for C.J. and Gigi)	83
April is the Mother Month	84
Raggedy Ann Rhymes and Silly Putty Jewels (for Vicki)	85
Bringing Apples Down	86
Hear Ye!	91
Earthward	92
Oh Precious Morning	93
Paths	94
Upon the Hearth	95
Mid-June	96
Captains	97
Ohio	98
Review Questions	101

Appendix A

Poetry Primer	103

Appendix B

Acknowledgements	115
About the Author	117
Epilogue	119
Photo "With Papa"	121

Oh god, Papa

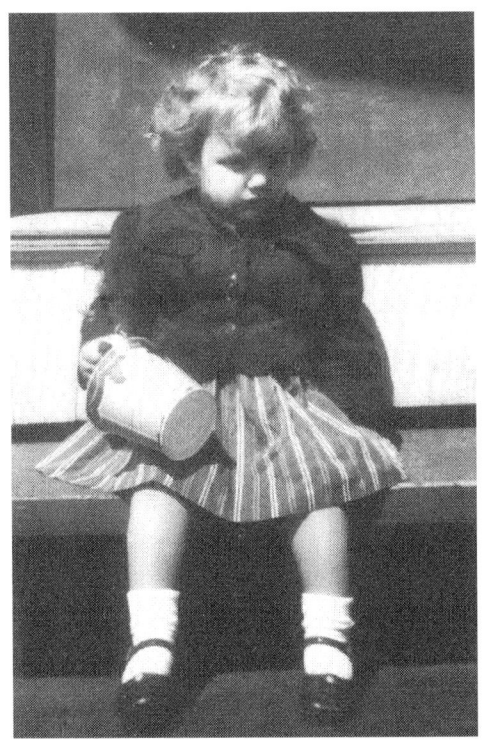

Marking Time

Every month when my body begins to bloat,
I think of you pudding-faced and fish-eyed
marking the calendar "friend coming."

Back when I was half-baked, I dusted
your collection of dime store knick knacks
every uneventful Saturday.
And every uneventful Saturday,
no plummy, mustachioed man
with Roman nose and set jaw
came to make the task worthwhile.

Still, your China cupboard waited
with its dreams of Hummels and Haviland—
dark and empty like you. Meanwhile,
I polished the boy and girl who'd lost
their Dutch features through chemical peels
of Fantastic and Pledge, two statues
distinguished only by their "S" and "P."
Slow, deliberate movements of time
marked Saturdays, months, years.
I had the pronounced "s" that made you wince.
You had the steely voice from Steubenville streets.
My "s" and your steel clashing like swords—
fencing with little conversation.
I ran out of hope and polishing cloths.

You continued to mark time, "friend coming,"
while the knick knacks mimicked you
cob-webbed and worn.

I didn't know it was your period
you waited for each month
to prove you were still a woman—
to foster some faint hope
of the man from Pittsburgh
coming in his Cadillac
to fill your cupboard,
empty
all these years,
with the priceless gift
I could never hope to be.

Knowing

Daddy swings his dagger-hoe
side-by-side with hired help.
Together, like mad warriors,
they flail, slash the air,
slice the ground, flail again.
"Damn things," they curse,
"we'll starve if this keeps up!"

Who could have known this day
would come to claim the belt
that Daddy used to whip the world?
Self-reliance holds steady hands
to the Midwest plow, but that same
fortitude puts blood in the land
if you love it too much—
and Daddy does.

Nebraska notions brought him here;
Nebraska notions will take him home—
underground where the Ogallala sings
a lullaby from Omaha to Odessa.
Corn rows bow, brown flags wave—
tokens of surrender from a lesser god.
A sullen scarecrow views the scene—
arms outstretched: a fitting sacrifice.

Putting By

It happened one day when she was putting pickles
by—the Gherkin type,

thumb-size and nubby. She was at the sink
scrubbing fuzz from pickle skins when

she collapsed forward onto the drain board, then
backward to the Spic and Spanned floor.

We looked on in horror as she lay there,
pickle brush still clutched

in her hand like it was the wand
of a fairy godmother.

How many years had she stood at that chipped
porcelain farm sink working

herself red-faced and sweat-browed over a batch of
pickles, oceans of tomato sauce,

and green beans she canned every year, and every
year were greedily eaten?

We had the friends and family in, and showed her
pantry full of putting by—

as though the bright yellow peaches peeking from
the Mason jars were her, and not

the cold monument of flesh at the funeral home,
hands caught up around a lace

hankie. It was like something sacrilegious had
happened; she had never in her life

carried a lace hankie, always a serviceable men's
handkerchief. And around her

were too many roses drowning out the essence of
vinegar and herbs—the trademark of her practicality.

So instead, we gathered in the kitchen and hummed
her songs of putting by—the

ones she always sang as she traveled miles around
the gold-veined Linoleum where

we played like there would never be an end to her
lulling us. We opened her last

year's Gherkins and paid tribute with a collective
crunch and sigh.

There is honor in housewifing.
We hadn't always known.

Woodland Bird
for Gerard Manley Hopkins

"...Through the echoing timber does so rinse and wring
The ear, it strikes like lightnings to hear him sing..."
~ Gerard Manley Hopkins

The summoning sound of the woodland bird
Again the sound, and yet again it comes
About its primal way without discord
In rhythmic motion plays on nature's drums.
And so I pause to hear it from the ground
Rapping out its beat like nursery rhyme.
Gentler then, and gentler yet it comes around
Acting out its part staccato time.
I hear not one, but two—not two but three
Songs fall then rise into crescendo beats.
As Pan conducts the forest symphony,
The walnut woodsong falls to cedar seats.
It leaves it earthy echo in my ear
Drumming tunes to keep me ever near.

Apple Towns
for Dylan Thomas

In a '49 Ford heading for New York, I watch
as lights bring lines to life, moving them
forward like numbers on perpetual calendars.
I fluff chiffon around my knees and wait for you.

The radio pipes forth its canned quotation,
quite unlike your voice of '53,
"Rage, rage against the dying of the light!"
it said. "November 9th, Dylan Thomas is dead."

A primal cry breaks free devouring the dash,
the visor veils my brows with black for mourning,
glovebox gives no courtesy of Kleenex—empty
like this space I have that only you could fill.

Did you fight for life, did you rage at death?
Or was it natural—the completion of you, the
circle whose arc was struck at birth not long ago?
Could it be you're here with me, again, in '53?

Or are you, even now, easy under apple boughs
running like a boy again—you were the stranger
people wanted to take home, amuse, befriend.
Could it be, those expectations ended you?

Who, now, will wrap my sum of insecurities with velvet words—suspend them steel-strong over the abyss of life, and bring me grass-green happiness? Who now, my prince, will rule the apple towns?

Things that Stay

Possessions are the only things that stay:
treasures trapped in webs of time,
images held by rubber band hands.
She crouches among them—remnants
of the days when Mama, Papa, and
three siblings caught by four walls
learned love, tested tempers, sought solace.

She remembers Evening In Paris: the gift
for a Mother's Day—when was it: '45?
She lifts the ample box: five and dime cologne
enshrined in cobalt blue laid to rest
against a bed of silver. She runs a fragile finger
across the fish-like shapes.

They thought she loved the scent—
she never said otherwise. No matter;
she loves it now. It speaks of times before
the house seemed big, barn-like.
She dabs a bit behind her ears,
leans back against the rafters,
and swears she feels her Henry
touch her neck...softly.

Holding Fast

She stands stoically like some Greek goddess
Surveying her domain of Ohio green.
Refusing to bow to demi gods—us,
She peers across Mount Vernon's Route 13.
Who knew her first in 1823
When hopeful hands set her firm foundation?
Some say a Scotsman and his family
Summoned to a democratic nation.
Whose human hands, assisted in some way
By celestial god and goddess hosts,
Inspired her bricks of Midwest orchard clay
And laid her western walk and lintel posts?
Mere mortals dare to seal her urban doom,
But she holds fast for time to make her tomb.

Papa

When I was anxious with age,
a pea bursting and flaring its pod—
oh god, Papa,
so many times I tried to tell you
who I was, but now
you're side-by-side with Mama
and you have to listen.
Remember when I'd sit on your knee
and you'd force my hair locks around
your finger like the curls on grapevine runners,
and how you'd sit with your teeth vice-gripped
around your pipe stem
as I wore the fake fur stole
you bought me for Christmas?
You told me then
men could be trusted—
your actions told me, Papa.
I thought they'd be like you:
bolted to the beam of family devotion—
that if I was meek and mild
they'd be good to me.
I learned from you
my place was gingerbread and apron strings.
"Don't be bold and independent," you'd say.
But you never said I was different,
never mentioned I had a choice,
never told me I was like you.

It took me years, Papa, to become me—
to become you—
to have the grit you had
when you stalked the Copperheads
that lived in the cistern.
Do you remember?
You said when I grew up
another man would take your place.
Papa, you lied.

Sugar Creek
for the Amish

They weave the web of reason for the day.
She fills the lamps, he brings in wood, they eat,
By certain cautious conversation say
What must be said about the corn and wheat.
Tradition dictates what it is they know.
She trims the wick and flares the wax aside,
He works the field with mules, his plow in tow.
Their blues and blacks and browns will not confide.
On Sabbath day their faith can cool desire,
And hold them in the daylight hours—null.
At slipping down of sun, they lay the fire;
The chores complete, the kids asleep, moon—full.
They undo webs of reason for the night;
Unfold forbidden fruit by candlelight.

Enough

Looking up at leaves,
I find that I am satisfied
with simple green,
godly in its keeping me secure
belly up on the weathered swing.

So much can be said
of Holsteins leaning into hills.
The black and white
of things
make no mistake
of who you are,
where you're going,
where you're not.
The trail back to the barn
is brief.

And what about the lazy rye
sleeping under certain sun?
Tomorrow it will be there,
and I will walk slowly
to fetch the scythe.

Bloomingdale

In a place called Bloomingdale,
there should be no suffering.
But there was, so I took it with the oatmeal
and milk that tasted of wild garlic
our Jersey cow had eaten.
In the Bloomingdale of my imagination,
I rode a Palomino home to the safety of arms
that never tired of holding, lips that never
ceased to speak of love.

In reality, I got the Chestnut gelding, and on him
I rode hard, jumped fences to escape the Cape Cod
facade that held me prisoner for ten years.
Did they think their fences would make me stay—
there where staying meant insanity
wrapped in white—
aluminum happy face that lured
unwary visitors with its Judas welcome mat?

I read somewhere that most houses in America
are white, and so it is in Bloomingdale at least.
It makes me wonder if in all of those white houses,
people are prisoners, if they long to be free
of a place like Bloomingdale where there should be
no suffering.

Promise Like Stone

There's a headstone in a distant cemetery
that proves we have a mother.
Two names rest there, but only one sleeps.
Papa's date is blank because he's still alive
and living with some Susie half his age,
resisting the site like an
impatient man gone fishing.
And so we go as on a pilgrimage:
Mother's Day, Memorial Day,
and any other day three sibling-selves
can pack into a blue Chevy wagon
and trek to the tomb of the unknown mother.
The womb that warmed us waits.
We pull up weeds,
plant amaranths for immortality,
white roses for spiritual love and purity.
We add some salvias—her favorite.
It matters to us, even if the groundskeeper
will mow them down without remorse.
For us, there is solace in their sentiment,
so we do it loyally like so many chicks
shadowing a hen.
It is the only thing we know
of permanence: this place,
this placard promise of granite—
obligatory whetstone that sharpens

spiritual senses.
We trace her name with heavy hands,
say it aloud as though it brings her to us,
and it does.

In some small way we know her
because we have her here
in this distant cemetery
waiting for Papa
to bring again
red roses.

The Offering

The presence of man
insists on a John Deere tractor
chugging home
to the black and blatant
Mail Pouch barn.

Left behind, the great beige bales
pin the hills to the
pink horizon.
Under the full phase,
they come to life—
offer-up stubble and chaff,
dance to ancient
rhythms.

The mandatory moon
duplicates the beasts—moves
their shadows
west to east.

Seeing Red

You weren't who I expected
wearing your aura of My Sin perfume
like a helmet in '61.
I, drawn too soon from Mother's milk,
saw you in all your splendor
driving Daddy's Cadillac down
roads of dust, wooing him in red
while Kruschev and Castro
moved on main street—
onward to the cold war.

But God and I were talking
as you donned your mask of Maybelline.
You see, I had that little red Bible
the Gideons gave me,
back when prayer was still in school,
peace was cool, and 'Camelot'
moved and breathed in powerful harmony
—days before black was the color of Rose.

Believing crimson phrases
caught between a strip of satin
and the sweat of fingertips,
I curled myself in fetal comfort
and watched the cherry limbs
slap the windows season-to-season.
You fixed your lipstick and drove away.

Potatoes

Even as a child, I knew
Grandma was in denial.
Never would she forgive her God
for forcing her from the land she loved.
Never would she accept
the baptism of beef
America had so freely given her.

When Grandma told the story
of the Irish Potato famine,
she'd compare it to the testing of Job.
She'd cozy the teapot, and nestle into
some far away story that ended with
"but time heals all wounds."

She kept mementos from the old country—
a cross her mama clutched while her papa
gave his ghost fighting the famine,
a daguerreotype of the Irish family
standing near wide expanses of root crop fields—
prosperity pulling smiles easily.

In my mind, I see Great Grandpa
with his wagon stacked to rack's height
with potatoes.

An act of settling takes place
as the wagon rocks and reels over the narrow
trail, up and around the hills of God-green grass
and scarred gray rock face. By the time he gets
to market, the largest potatoes are on top.

Mr. O'Leary of O'Leary Mercantile fame
furrows his caterpillar brows while Grandpa
explains, "Leprechauns have done it—
tricksters that they are!" But not even leprechauns
could have saved Great Grandpa from the famine.

We ate potatoes every night.
Grandma said it was only fitting since we were Irish.
She wouldn't admit it was her way of spiting God—
the God that took her from that fair green country
where it is said the leprechauns still wait for wagons
listening for the crick and creek
of wooden wheels
groaning under a payload
of brown, beautiful
potatoes.

Broken Wing
for George Eliot

Dove with broken wing—
winter's response
to the spring in her heart.
She chooses a dream
of feathers and down
on an evening that's snow-sure.
The setting sun introduces the moon
at the opposite horizon—
seesaw game of all's well.
Balanced over the crystal ball of earth,
predicting future, the moon's aura
holds her captive
in a cave of evergreen.

Peaceful is her slumber.
She won't know
the frost of morning,
hear the chitter of sparrows
establishing their pecking order
at the Griff House feeder,
or see the old man coming to feed them—
his nose as red as the bucket which holds
the seed. Millet, sunflower, thistle
dwindling down reluctantly.

Layers of Meaning

like the parfaits you used to make
when we were children,

like chiffon over crinolines
in summer when other children
were wearing shorts,

and snowsuits over pants
long before the snow.

"How time flies!" you'd say.
But what you really meant was
youth had flown

no matter how you tried
to wrap it, save it, preserve it
vicariously through us.

Layers of meaning—
like medicine for the well.

Old Joe
for John Steinbeck

Outside, calves bawl and beg
inside the safeness of their stalls.
Celia pulls a chair and pours coffee.

Old Joe says, "Ain't much pickin' this year
'cuz a the drought." He shoves empty hands
into empty pockets.

"I done California last year.
Went plum to Washington state
'fore I's finished. But not this year
'cuz a the drought."

"Why do they call you Old Joe?" Celia asks,
lifting her coffee cup and feeling for a donut.
"You can't be more than forty?" She busies
her hands with various chores
while her eyes rivet to the steely gray of his.

He lifts his hat, scratches his head
for concentration, "Been nigh-on 20 years
I been pickin'. Reckon that's why they call me
Old Joe. Gets in yer blood—don't know why,
jus' do."

Outside the bawling continues.
Buckets clank against worn trouser legs.
Celia watches as Old Joe boards the wagon,
listens as the tractor spits 'all aboard'
shouts of smoke.
She pushes herself from the doorway, starts her
list of things to do, but something in the way
Old Joe saw things had her wanting to hear more.
Beyond the kitchen window,
calves nurse udders contentedly.

The Girl Who Peed Her Pants

Blonde and beautiful like I wasn't,
you were who I longed to be.
If eye color were an option,
I'd have chosen yours.
But you were frail and pale
like some small ghost
torn between two worlds.

I had empathy for you the day
you peed your pants. It was clear
no one else did, standing in that
God forsaken music line
banging tambourines, singing
"As I was strolling through
the park one day...cha cha cha."
If there had been a park in Pleasant Hills,
we wouldn't be strolling through it
banging tambourines!

I've held my anger against that teacher
all these years for not allowing you
the restroom. Who was she
to judge your discomfort level?
Your name I can't remember,

but I'm sure it was something fragile
like Tina or Lisa, quite unlike
my stout German name.
What you must have suffered
because you could not control your bladder,
and what I have suffered
having to remember it for you.

Perhaps you've moved away
to some fair place where no one knows
you peed your pants in first grade.
Me—I moved away, changed my hair,
took a pretty French name.

I guess the lesson here is
that we can have contempt for ourselves
no matter what. And we just keep strolling,
banging our tambourines, looking for that
perfect park where there are no urges,
no needs, no pains.

Loosening
for Walt Whitman

Let me walk in tall grass
in unencumbered, cool clothes,
in white and soft, fresh linen
into morning's new dew.

No One's Princess

I'm looking at the roses you never brought
in a vase on a table of my imagination,
weeping blue into amber crackle glaze
like the shattered emotions never tidied up
by you. No fairytale resolutions.

Feeling like Cinderella after midnight:
half-garbed, eager for a tete-a-tete
within the white splendored circumference
of golden bands. You outgrew yours.

Hearing still, small voices
like velvet hammers on my soul
trying to please that father deep within:
the one who never said
I was a princess.

Game Show Salvation

No more shrouds of Turin!
No fool's gold of stigmata
to dupe us to devotion.
Give us God—
real as razor burn!

Be gone false messiahs
in blue knit suits.
No more goose pimple passion
from electronic pulpits.
Only the Christ will do.

Jesus of Nazareth, come on down!

A Well

Divining rod of willow branch
—curious little man
withered like October corn,
weathered like the earth is weathered,
brown of hands and brown of branch
becoming one.

He caresses the air in foreplay
until the willow rod bends in agony
toward the dark thighs of earth.

A girl of ten should doubt some things,
seek scientific explanations.
"Prove it!" I demanded.

"A well is proof enough,"
he said to me that day—
his words, like waterfalls,
spilling into future.

Willows
for *Midwest farmers*

I remember willows
bending toward ground
like Papa after chores.

Through their shifting leaves,
strains of "Swing Low, Sweet Chariot"

dipping,
swaying—pendulums
sweeping
time.

The Gathering at Emerson's
for Ralph Waldo Emerson

I am but this: a shadow-elf
of that grand home he knew himself.
My ivy's swirling, curling rise
was godly greeting for his eyes
and those of that brief circle then
who came to sup and sit within
his hallowed walls and drink his wine
and read from Wordsworth,
poems divine.

Their echoes still, a vigil keep,
"...the very houses seem asleep..."

Then Whitman read from *Leaves of Grass*
while brows were raised with tip of glass.
He kept on reading, touching those
who had not heard a poem as prose,
and thus a new comrade was born
after midnight—before the morn.
I was there as a witness first
to hear the best, to hear the worst—
to watch as boys came up to men
and 'round about to boys again!

I knew them all; their pens were swords.
My hallway sounded with their words
that found their way to heart and mind,
and left their mark on all mankind.
New footsteps trace my halls each day
while nimble fingers dust away—
I am but house, and not a home,
to mark the map, display the tome.

I do not wish in history's eye
to be a shrine to passers-by.
But let me be to hear the sound:
familiar echoes underground.
Allow my frame to go to dust
And all within to mold and rust.

Alas, as it was meant to be—
I with the masters, they with me.
Ah yes—they were a bunch back then
who won the world with heart and pen,
and lucky, I, to have been home
to such as they of prose and poem.

Harmony

The soul
   the foot is wearing
   does not diminish
   with the walk,
   but springs on eager wings
   to become the hawk.

The soul
   selects a melody for two.
   Though heard by only one,
   it bears the burden
   of truer sounds
   thrumming at the drum.
   The natural ear
   cannot hear
   a truth as deep as this—
   betrays itself
   with a single,
   silent hiss.

The soul
   the hand is wearing
   feels the moment to be thrust,
   yet lets it slip
   with certainty
   when it must.

Universal Rhythm

Run to the rhythm of deerhide drumbeats—
forward and away to evergreen arms
pungent with ancient Algonquin echoes.

Enter the damp husk of red remembrance
where time turns to meet itself
like a swallow's sharp angle against
the drawn shades of evening sky.

Feel the repetitive rhythm
of the universe—contractions
deep within a womb
ready for the steady hands of midwife.

Dream of your brother, the white man,
milking the earth mother to extinction
in neat, measured increments of time
and time and time again.

Apocalypse

"The dishes need cleared," I say.
The maid comes—no purpose but
to please her Master.
The twisted fettuccine sticks
like hungry arms of dying loved ones
to plates they passed down
before they went. She scrapes them
with due sacred propriety.
Armories of ashtrays house bullets
from last night's warfare on mankind.
She spills the contents without mercy,
shoving with practiced finger
on a resistant stub that begs to stay
like a bad habit.

She says something in a monotone,
sounds like a Hail Mary.
"Are you doing penance?" I ask.
She nods and continues.
"You should too," she returns.
"They find things in Middle East...
not so good, you know?"
She turns her gaze back to dinnerware
glazed over with pesto sauce,
scrubbing with whole heart
as though her last duty.

She continues her chanting,
"Hail Mary, Full of Grace…"
I watch as the first light of morning
oozes through the valance above—
a light that some would kill for.

On 66 Heading West
for Jack Kerouac

It's sort of how you look at a thing
with eyes half closed
that makes it what it is—
the way heat waves sift sunset reds
through black and baited lashes.
It was our first adventure
when we called the road home.
Never were good at domestic things:
calling hogs, calling auctions,
calling when we'd be late. Daddy said
we should, and so we didn't.

Didn't want to be like them with
eyes wide open, living life knowing
they would someday turn up toes
and die. We were smarter than that
with our stash of denials in traveling
bags heading west to find what folks
call no man's land.

Just what we were looking for through
half-lidded squints of gray-green
offered up by our friendly Wayfarers.
There is no death when the radio spits
jazz from Daddy's dashboard radio.

On 66 heading west, we went
unused by fame, war, work,
politics—two, maybe three
tearing up the road with the
stick shift tightly in hand as
though it controlled the world.
And it did.

Talking

I was talking today
and as I talked,
your gaze was on
inanimate things:
a table, a lamp,
a chair. Such silly
lifeless gods to be
holding your attention
instead of me.
They will be here
when I am
gone.

Soul Brown

The spiritual hands of man move earth—
battlegrounds of life, death. He converts
the fallow field, warring weeds
that tooth sod like kids clinging to mothers.
In their place go anointed seeds. He tucks
each one in a fatherly way, daring to defy
the black of crow and starling. He rolls each
seed from the palm of his hand outward
with his thumb to his index finger, skillfully
pinching the seed. The mounds are measured
with his size ten shoe, just about a foot.

He performs the ritual of brown—
soul brown like the eyes of a martyr,
like the brown of monks' robes
simple, yet purposeful.
The ritual ends with the water blessing.
He waits. He watches. The hungry sun
sucks reds from flannel shirts and neckerchiefs,
forces brown on his bold, bare hands.
Hovering like an expectant father,
sealed in a shroud of sunstream, he reaches
to touch the gold of green.

Mother

Her back is an arch
bent over the world—
protective dome of mother.
She leans forward—
her simple apron
folds in years around her.

She moves on bended knees
scrubbing the world white
like her cotton pinafore,
like her face in sunstream,
like her prayers going up
for clueless children.

Nature Within
for Thomas Merton

His head is a neat knob

carrying Kentucky ridges

and fields he'd traversed

through friendly mother folds

surrounding Gethsemani Abbey.

The stout nose mirrors the strength

of Gethsemani herself.

His eyes—pure pools

from Kentucky springs.

Brows—open abbey gates.

A cross stitches its way

between them,

forming horizontal and vertical

cross braces of the man.

His lips are silent altars of sacred greeting.

The smile akin to the spread wings

of a nectar-euphoric butterfly.

His teeth—worn white monuments—

crosses in Cistercian soil.

The strong chin and cheekbones—

the walls that held him.

The full jaw—soft,

yet firm in its fatherly way.

His dimples are deep and unrelenting—

childhood's unforsaken hold.

Hair—whisper-sparse

like common poverty grass.

The stark cowl and scapular juxtaposes

the mellow features of the man

like a mat and frame.

His ears seem soft and open

to a harsh world, saucers holding secrets—

aural avenues for the Sapphic sounds

of Kentucky rural life.

Trapped willingly, enshrined forever

and inseparable from the man himself.

Vespers deep in a valley—

the caw of crow, the cracking ice

breaking the river's thread

through Vineyard Knob,

the rounded ring of abbey bell,

lively laughter of creek bottom kids,

the baptismal buzz of honeybees

on fallen fruit—their wings like lace

in the flirting sun.

Etude in White
for Emily Dickinson

Who can doubt the white welcome of sheets

fresh from dancing pas de deux

across a darker line of sky—

flipped and tucked and fresh as

French maids in morning white pinafores?

Who can resist a lady Ivory-scrubbed

and poet-shirted?

Softly coos the dove—how quiet is her lover.

Let the unsaid say more

by pale suggestion.

Becoming

Today, I'm not who I was,
nor will I be again.
Intimately tucked beneath
new commitments
are old flannels—comfortable.
I wait like haunched hind legs
of cats for reactions to my actions.

Yesterday I was,
but really wasn't
who I was.
Today I am who I am,
and that's OK for now,
but tomorrow
I may grow away.

Faith

Rear views tell us all we need
to know of what is past.
Fireflies flashing S O S
deep in the flight of night
mimic repetitive prayers
from lips of mothers who had
begged us to stay.

But there is life out there—
beyond this now, and that then.
Saint Anthony stares from a
dashboard clip.

We wrestle with our spirits
like Ezekiel's wheel which pulls
our future, a resigned
compass pointing anywhere
but home—anywhere but there
"sweet chariot,"
where life is normal.

Ignored

What does it matter
that men don't notice you?
They are occupied noticing
themselves.

It is far better
to be ignored

than to live indebtedly—
to be with faces in a crowd,
be nothing, and yet be proud—
say nothing, and yet be loud.

Colors of America
for U.S. patriots

These are the colors of America flying
high above the jagged summit of man's desire.
We see them when we pass each courthouse,
statehouse, or patriotic papa's Sohio station.
Flags, like battle banners, bring crowds to
baseball games, tennis matches, and boat races.
During an evening drive, we see them arched
and whipping against the false light of street lamps.
They remain like lighthouses of hope for all
who pass beneath on streets of color—
the colors of America.

NEVER!

It was the angry feel of "Never!"
that brought us here—to
this unwinding of the 'we.'
No one has the right to speak
"Never!" to another. It is a word
too full of rage and power.

Some compromise the inner self to deal
outside themselves—to fracture the truth
enough to make it livable,
bendable, acceptable.
I never imagined and never will imagine
being contented with "Never!"

The only truth I know is that
I'm never going back, back, back
to the way he said "Never!" and
the way I felt "Never!" when he said it.

Sirens

A young man died today.
Sirens rang their shrill alarm
through a still and folded city night.
Cereal box buildings bore the shadow-flash
of crimson light—crazed artist manipulating
a mop-like brush across the city's
black canvas.

"He was just a youth," came a clearly tired voice.
"Just seventeen," adds another.
"Bound to happen in this neighborhood!"
they say in agreement.
The clash of steel against steel delivers the
message of death—cold as the cadaver in the street.

They turn, walk, shake their heads.
Two streets down, a voice oozes from the
oil-thick night, "She was only fourteen!"
Another chimes in, "Shouldn't have been out
this time of night."
"Bound to happen in this neighborhood!"
they say in unison.

And So We Write

Since the beginning of recorded time,
everything we know or believe to be true
we learn from prose and poetry.
We are the sum total of: books of scholars,
studies of scientists, sonnets of Shakespeare,
scrolls of scribes, clay cuneiform of Assyrians,
upright steles of Moabites, potsherds of
Samaritans, Coptic codices of Egypt,
Septuagint of Greece, epic poems of bards.

A writer writes it; a poet perfects it;
a journalist lives it. This awesome duty
keeps poesy pumping from pens,
fiction leaping from laptops,
reports rap-tapping onto 8 ½ by 11,
20 pound paper.

We are the next narrative heroes,
the narcotic tenth muse.
And so we write:
the poems that pulse the planet,
the rhyme that rocks the orb,
the history of man's hedonism,
the who, what, when, where, why—
the never-ending manuscript of life.

Armies of Salvation

Out of the '60s and
competing in the '70s race,
we pulled our pockets inside out
and looked hungry for our meals.

The "Will Work for Food" signs
kept us for awhile. Nuns loved us
and gave us homilies galore.
The Armies of Salvation made us work,
and so we printed more signs.

"The Government Did This to Us!"
The tires screeched with their stopping.
There was no end to the offers we got
by relating to the world what the world
knows best.

Our most productive sign was the red
lettered one that shouted truths
too close to home,
"Most Americans are only a few
paychecks away from being homeless!"
That one got us chicken and dumplings
and spare basement bunks.

Linoleum

Lately I feel like old Linoleum—
the kind you find in '40s and '50s houses—
gold veins etching out green and blue.

It came to me suddenly at 35.
Tired of the obvious lack of care Linoleum gets,
I realized I'd become a fixed pattern—
the 'who it is' they think I am—
playground dutied to the punishment of family feet.

One day, I'll become disposable.
They'll cry awhile for the nostalgia of it.
They'll say, "Do you remember when…?"
They'll lay in my place tiles designed to look new
twice as long—no special care required.

Half-Light
long poem

Ladies lean from windows yearning for slices
of solitude, getting only half moon.
Tomorrow, they'll pull their kids half-dressed
half-loved to a mission in downtown
Columbus for free coats.

Here in tenements 1-200, decisions are for
putting off until the next life what you should
be doing now. For 101, life is food stamps,
ADC, and chunks of government cheese.
Children with their half-smiles
will bring her satisfaction for the day.

She says nothing.
There is nothing to share that will make
things different. Tonight they will see her,
leaning out of the window, over the edge,
trying to bring Columbus to herself.

The cityscape blinks hypnotic messages across
LaVec Tower, lays a cautious wash of light
across the rooftop of Franklin County Jail.
Nearby, German Village summons those who
search for yesteryear with its sausage haus,
brick streets, and gartens seen in slick mags.

The exit ramp from I-70 is lit up like OSU.
The steady white-upon-green brings travelers
into her midst like Israelites entering the green
of promised land.

101 has memories of half-light dropping like stars
from a bruised and purple sky. She relives them
nightly. Here in the city of opportunity, capital,
hub, center of the universe, she is just a number
HUD gave to her, welfare knows her by, and ADC
uses to identify her children. They are numbers too.

Somewhere in sync with so many footsteps,
beating-out a runaway rhythm, is the man
who took her halfway there, then split.
And halfway through the night, she will dream him
into a charming wholeness of man: bringing
paychecks home, hugging legitimate children,
taking her to heights where half-love has no ticket.

Just before she rises in the false pink morning,
she looks at the blanket-draped windows and wishes
for full light. She remembers the Scripture from a
bag lady's Bible, "I am the Light and the Life..."
She reaches for the lamp switch. No light today.

Hers at birth, the generational curse: this life, this
place, these children cycled through her
nine months times three with brief pauses in
between. She can't blame him—out there

half-drunk, flirting with some half-witted
woman who buys his story.

Half-lidded, half-shadowed by the window ledge
of 126 above, she rakes her hair with rigid fingers,
a nervous habit she learned for coping early on.
She has half a mind to jump, but half-way down
she'd likely change her mind, and so she doesn't.

Above her, 126 leans over to see if 101 is out and
leaning. "Get yer kid's coats yet? Catch Guiding
Light t'day? Had ta go ta Cleveland Avenue on the
COTA bus. Bus was late, kids was squawlin'!
Mercy!" There's a measured pause. "Almost the 1st.
Got some coupons fer Krogers. Bring 'em down
tomorra. Mebbe catch Guiding Light at yer place.
Jus ain't right how he up 'n left ya."

126 asks and answers her own questions; it's safer
that way in the 'hood. 101 remains long enough to
bathe herself in half-light. Somwhere out in that
pulse of rhythmic city lights, there is someone else
dying to be whole. She embraces the thought,
slumps into bed.

A half-lit neon sign flashes mercilessly across her
stretch-marked belly, her sagging breasts, her vein-
purpled thighs—blinking-out the message she knows
too well—the whole truth.

Passage

Ships of blue on seas of white,
a marriage of words laid full
on muslins meant for Sunday only.
I stifle silent screams—
caught words aching to be freed
like amniotic fluid against
a womb full of birth.
Tradition anchors me
in the still,
      safe,
           waters...
                  (Exit the gods)

I steer out to "see"
against the status quo,
flounder against nets
meant for martyrdom—
the fresh mist of morning
and Mt. Helicon just ahead.
Ambition urges me
into the raging,
        doubtful,
             current...
                    (Enter the gods)

A Gordon
for Lord Byron

Aberdeen called you forth—the mist that
night like a bay harbor hag. Oh fated one,
you hopeless romantic, you were too bright
a candle in your dark world—a world gone
mad for science and fact.

Two hundred years too late for love,
I open your words—burn wounds
upon my soul. I love you for your heart my
Lord, not for your flesh which consumed you.
I, like Dante's Beatrice, would have freed you
from the whores, the wars, the hell! You, Lord
of the Gordons, I have never loved…so well.

Valeur du Temps
Value of Time

If I could know you in another time,
we would be lovers
meeting in the gardens at Sainte Adresse
watching the gay ragatta as Monet captured us
on canvas—eternal bliss.

Perhaps we'd stroll through the Parc Monceau,
or put up in a chateau near Marsailles—soft
sea air parting the curtains as we sleep.
But, alas, there is only now.

When?
for D.H. Lawrence

At 5:00, I come to you—
my apron full of bright fruits
to break bread.

With my laughter and easy
conversation, I touch places in you
that you have never known.

Willows sway us into childish notions:
arms, legs, up, down—rhythmic celebration
on the old rope swings.

We relax into the sunset.
I bathe your feet and dry them
with my waist-length hair.

I taste your lips and find a hint
of jasmine tea. You listen to my poetry.
I savor your hunting songs.

We become one in nature's silken web
under Eros' spell, under the veiled sky—
too shy to expose us.

The veil parts.
You walk alone to a small cottage
and wait.

Somewhere Down the Road

Safe in California
from a two year life in holding—
holding on to dreams in brown paper bags
and tapestry satchels, they come—their
only purpose is to live—here where they *can* live.
I look out over San Diego,
where Cabrillo found his Spanish fame.
I try to see it the way they see it—
like Cabrillo did in the new world.
Yet, I know I cannot know
the way they see it
because it is already mine.
The bone-bare immigrants smile toothless smiles,
clutch bags and slender-bellied children
to them, step to sacred ground.
Somewhere down the road, someone
will tell of this time. It will be written down,
passed-down, melted-down through the
American melting pot.
I turn my face from the scene
and back to bay reality—freeway just ahead.

All Lucy-Like in Narnia
for C.S. Lewis

The wardrobe fairies fancy cordial wine,
but Mister Tumnus keeps with his disguise
and serves his tea all hot and honey-fine
while Lucy falls asleep to her demise.
She wakens with a sigh—oh grief to know
that truth can be as sinful as a lie.
The frocks of fools are slippery like snow.
Oh blinding fate, oh faunish tale—oh fye!
Yet pulling back the cloak her life has worn,
Lucy laughs aloud at dresses torn.

The Color of Pain

I speak to you in black words
of black tears, of black pains.
My words hang deathless:
your race—my race;
white face—black face.
I long to be as you—
to be whole inside.
My lips are full and softened
from my salt streams.
They quiver to speak the words,
"I love you, human being," but
they do not, will not—are not
expected to say friendly words.
My hands long to touch yours—
To mingle our sweat,
to blind us both to prejudice.
Close your eyes and your mind.
Can you feel my black hands—
my black sweat?
"I love you. I understand." Say my lips,
but "No," says my mouth.
Someday, I'll—we'll say it,
and the world will follow our example.

Man is a Farmer

Man is a farmer.
He rides his proverbial tractor
into the fields of life
and spreads his bullshit
far and wide
until the sun sets
on his weeded ways.

Indestructible

Facing north, I feel you move beneath me. Your great oak planks underfoot, and deep inside the sense of sturdy
future.

The night air allows a Kingfisher space for his song—a rhythmic trilling sound like the trickling Mohican beneath his perfect perch of spotted sycamore.

Summoning my spirit like so many times before in childhood secrets—pulling me like the saltwater taffy that held together tender moments of my youth.

I held the sweetness until duty led me away, and yet—here I am many years hence on this trail of native dreams—this monument here and now just for me—just for this night and forever.

Something about the tenacity of the age-old bridge, about the ancient Indian river, about the sounds that come from below and move easily across the valley—natural as the night air around me—
indestructible

as Indian legend, obvious as the oak—our existence interwoven like the great Mohican trails. Facing south, you call my spirit once again, and fill my emptiness like the deep mysterious woods— wild and wondrous with the magic of your making.

Not So Solitary
For Henry David Thoreau

I baked bread today—
something I hadn't done since you
left the valley. It seemed there was
a purpose to it all when you were here.
Your expectations were the thread in our
unraveled tapestry.

I ate the bread alone.

I went to the woods
and noted bullfrogs in the pond—they
noticed me. Their loud eruptions
reminded me of you. A red-winged
butterfly sat on my shoulder.
His weight was nothing
compared to yours.

I took off my shoes and walked with God.

Who Yer Mama?

Who yer Mama, little one? Where she at,
and why ya out so late?

Who yer Papa, little one? Where he at,
and why ya carry dat heavy load?

Who yer people, little one? Where dey at,
and why ain't ya home for suppa?

Who yer friends, little one? Where dey at,
and why ain't ya hangin wit' em?

Who yer god, little one? Where he at,
and what will he do to save ya?

What yer song, little one? And why
ya up and dancin?

What dat ya say, little one? "Ya's full of Jesus
and a 'by God' attitude!" Mercy!

Git on home!

Libre Spiritus
Free Spirit

I felt your presence in your absence—a spirit free
and floating
around me. I went on bare feet, loosened my hair
from the
bondage of pins and let my golden tendrils bounce
mid-back.
I went in white among the evergreens calling your
name—
You are elusive, playing your game of cat and mouse.

I hear echoes tugging on my ear: children's voices
and laughter
and Mother calling home. Shall I heed the mother's
voice?
I remain like a nymph in the forest. My head is light,
my heart
is pounding. All of my senses are heightened like
some
drug-induced state.
The laughter continues; I am summoned
to a clearing
where your spirit lingers like the heavy odor of
honeysuckle.
I lie down and listen to the child in me,
giving up
innocently to the dance of the spirits.

I was asleep—but now—each molecule of me
awakens.
I'm floating above the matters of day, of time,
of circumstance. I shall never be alone again—here
in this green
and golden universe surrounded by footmen fairies
and imaginary carriages.
I need no other to prove I am a princess.
Somehow, I've known it all along.

I float like feathers up and down and up again with
no resistance—free
at last of the dull, aching duties of earth, guilt,
obligations,
free of anything but love.

The Yellow Piano

I passed your house the other day and saw
your old piano on the porch. There it was
in yellow splendor begging for a play.

You must have found a sale on yellow paint,
and thought you'd use a barn brush for the job.
But it made you by-God happy! You stopped short
of a smiley face and stickers though.

Now as it goes, tradition holds pianos brown or
black, certainly not goldenrod. But will a dull piano
somehow do when an old barn brush begs lemon
yellow hue?

The neighbors brought lawn chairs or sat cross-
legged in the yard to hear you play. Every round was
like the last, "Please don't take my sunshine away…"

The yellow piano punctuated the neighborhood—
pathetic with paintless clapboard houses and a
tumble down church.

The sermon was right there with lemonade and
gingersnaps, and ladies in broad-brimmed garden
hats—yellow of course.

Up the street, I heard a chorus singing. The whole town turned out like it was Christmas. Some voices old and shaking like their knees—some others sharp and full soprano.

"You are my Sunshine, my only Sunshine. You make me happy when skies are gray. You'll never know, dear, how much I love you. Please don't take my sunshine away."

Steel Town Blues
for Steubenville

The smoke stacks puke their guts into an empty parking lot. A red trail of dust outlines the billboard—wanton woman with cigarette. I light one up just to feel something in common.

We share a smoke together—the steel town, the billboard, and me. Our puffing takes on a blues like rhythm. "Just sittin' at the dock of the bay watchin' the tide roll away."

The blue-black Ohio adds to the mood with her tug boats and barges likes lines of military men going for rations: duty, survival, sacrifice.

Faux Pas

Sometimes I wear a white dress
when floating social seas of
basic black—looking
perfectly incorrect.

Ride home alone if it pleases you.

Celtic K(not)
for William Butler Yeats

Don't go there—where Yeats is the poet's heart
And the shamrocks are footstools from heaven.
Don't go little lassie; lad don't depart—
Keep your hearts in the shire of Devon.
Don't go there—to Ireland where half-doors are
Open and mantels hold pictures of love—
Where musty men and the red earthen floors
Heel hard with simplicity from above.
Don't go there—deep in the forest lilies
Leap up beside the forget-me-not.
And the green of the hillocks is like Dilly's
Pub where part of you lives like a knot.
    Still—Ireland calls you with pipes and with reels,
    And Gaelic songs to kick up your heels.

To the Pizza Shop Lady

She gazes in silent content creating gray boxes

from flats at the counter in DiCarlo's Pizza.

"For heaven's sake," I ask,

"why are you doing this to yourself?"

"Doing what?" she returns.

"I'm not doing anything."

"Exactly," I mumble, walking away

to the register.

I check my Daytimer for the flight schedule,

dig for a credit card, watch a run destroy

my hose down to the calf of my right leg.

"Damn! Meeting a client in an hour!

and my skirt is too short to hide the run!

My hairdo is all wrong...and"

But something draws my attention

back to her as she pushes the loose strands

of mousy hair back into its mother load.

It falls again. She ignores it

and continues to fold boxes,

stacking them in four neat rows side-by-side

allowing them them the touch of

fluorescent lights—a warmth

that only gray can kill.

She pulls her cardigan with the button

missing third down from the top,

adjusts it securely around her backside

before the baker sees her femininity.

It's not allowed—not now, not EVER.

"What an oddity." I think to myself. The baker shoves pizza rounds into squares covering them like fathers tucking children. She looks on in approval, doing the motherly thing.

"Have a nice day," she says

through a show of time-worn teeth.

I return the same. She says, "I will."

I have no doubt that what she says is true.

I close my cluttered purse

and rush away.

When Fall Apples Fall

When fall apples fall and leaves turn to rust.
When the spring paint is fading and the garden
is dust. The scarecrow is shivering, likely I figure
while out in the garden his pumpkins get bigger.
The hay mow looks like big Mr. Brown.
The melons are bursting out on the ground.
I sit inside a haystack hole, and with an apple
like a mole, I contemplate what winter brings
when fall apples fall and autumn winds sing.

Teddy Bear and Mr. Clown
for C.J. and Gigi

The rise and fall of mother's breast,
the strong embrace of father's chest
enfolded here in quilted down
with Teddy Bear and Mr. Clown.

The words of softness spoken here
for goodness of a life endear.
Slumber falls as night itself.
We put our cares up on a shelf.

In dreams we wrap our busy heads
and drift to heaven in our beds
where laughs and smiles are all around
with Teddy Bear and Mr. Clown.

Then mornings come as mornings must.
We waken to faces we love and trust.
Daylight will find us without a care
with sunshine streaming in our hair.

While running there as birds in flight,
we choose our dreams for another night.
Then laughingly we lay us down
with Teddy Bear and Mr. Clown.

April is the Mother Month

April is the mother month
giving birth to nature's whims.
So unlike any other month
when the metamorphosis begins.

April swelled with life-giving rain
pushing forth buds down wooded lane
when the leaves show their veins
up to the sky and softly wave
at passers-by.

April is the mother month.
It holds to its breast the calling bird
as chipmunks play in mossy trunk.
So is spring—born of rain in meadow heard.

Raggedy Ann Rhymes and Silly Putty Jewels
for Vicki

Life goes on—
you with your silly putty jewels
and play dough dolls,
and outside the weighted, waiting flowers
grow uneasy with their pollen for the bees.
You sing tunes of plump smiling pumpkins
and Raggedy Ann rhymes.
A new day breaks, and then the drowsy sun
tucks into the hills in a pretty purple blanket.
The popcorn clouds and all-day lime sucker
trees are there and always will be.
The grass awaits—cushions for your headstands,
somersaults, and leap frog fun.
The grasshoppers frisk
and woolly worms dance.
The dew calls you from vanilla bricks.
The hillside is roly-poly and daisy-dappled.
Rope swings toss with fairytale riders.
And life goes on.
So have your dreams. Fear not of today
for tomorrow is near at hand.
Jolly times await. There will always be
Raggedy Ann rhymes, Silly Putty jewels,
all-day lime sucker trees,
and you and me.

Bringing Apples Down

When days were long and nights

were made for sleeping, we sought

the succulence of apples

before their prime.

Preferring apple pie fate

to the munching and mooing

of Holsteins,

the apples clung for life

to the arms of the gnarled pasture trees

waiting for us to capture them.

It was a time of chivalry—our quest: the light green

perfect orbs hung heavenward.

Being a precocious pair,

we devised methods for conquering

the various family trees:

the Johnathans, the Macintoshes,

the gutsy Granny Smith,

and the most famous of the bunch,

Ida the Red! Our first method,

pelting the trees with fallen apples,

proved to be displeasing to the bees.

So we freed a board from the pasture gate

and proceeded to fence with the branches.

"On guard!" we'd shout. But our only success

was getting the cows to wander from

the orchard to investigate the broken gate.

When desperation set in,

you climbed the trunk and shimmied

out a limb. Splayed like a skydiver

against the stubbornness of upright limbs

and black bark, you rode the tree.

On the ground, I was the 'watch'

leaping over stationary ground troops

like a sorcerer.

Then the quest was over.

There it was: green and royal.

Like a sacred object, I polished it

on Levi legs and climbed the limb

where you were still wretching from the ride.

You sat upright and retrieved a chunk

of cow salt from your rolled-up t-shirt sleeve.

Just as there were methods of felling apples,

we had methods of eating them.

The best way was to take a bite, spit it out,

rub cow salt on the bitten part,

suck the juice, and bite again.

We sat for hours supporting our backs

on those generous limbs, legs stretched

in front of us for balance The sun decided

when it was time for us to gather the spoils

of the day and present them to the queen.

Remember when you, Robin the hood, donned

round green biceps, and I, Marion the maid,

created apple orb breasts?

I'm forty now. What I would give for those firm apple breasts. The trees—they disappeared long ago like you.

Hear Ye!

He festers inside—mad paper boy riveting meanings on headlines. "Hear ye!"

The culmination of wars past and present makes him anxious to change the world.

He isn't like the world though; his trousers are much too loose like those of the Jesus freaks of the '70s.

He reads beat poetry—recites his own on occasion when trash cans will listen.

Ashbery and Ginsberg are heroes calling attention to atrocities. "Hear ye!" But none do.

He slips into the night, and a new crier enters. "Hear ye, hear ye! Clean up in New York. Death toll rises!"

Hear ye?

Earthward

I want to be like God and recreate the world—

the wood, the wave, the mountain peak

that juts the sagging sky

and sees our fate like Noah saw

on Ararat so bleak.

If I could parent all the world, I would—with common sense, with love, with brotherhood.

Oh Precious Morning

Dewdrops drench the cherry leaves. Breezes blow up through the eaves.

Fickle scent of lilac fair sweeps away, then lingers there.

When light come peeking through the shade, and grass is sporting the color of jade—as

the red-winged blackbird sounds its warning, I'll be watching, oh precious morning.

Paths

Jaggers bow beside the moss

as if in conversation.

Mushrooms push their caps upright

beside the musty, hollow logs.

The creek lies rippling in

sandy beds.

May apples droop

as if they're napping.

Paths are worn from so much walking.

A 'No Trespassing' sign hangs

on a reluctant maple—its

wild and winged' seeds

spin down an invitation

just for me.

Upon the Hearth

Licking, singing, taunting flame—
   your beauty therein lies.

Upon the hearth, I'll curl with the cat while a
   cherry log spits and sighs.

A good meal and a cup of tea
is all I need except for this—

upon the hearth good company,
and a fire's fervid, ruby kiss.

Mid-June

The air is laden with summer scent. A halo embraces the moon.

Auspiciously calling, the bird as it went on sweetest of days in mid-June.

The climbing roses all but drip with sanguine color from God's brush.

Your two lips touch a glass of julep. The air sweeps softly as if to hush.

Your widely-brimmed hat nearly touches your nose. Your face, as the flowers, is in full bloom.

Cheeks with the hue of a blushing rose on the sweetest of days in mid-June.

The elm trees all but touch the clouds in reaching for the sky today. Flipping your brim, you laugh aloud.

Then turning your gaze to me, you say, "How well God has done his work today!"

Not much lovelier could it bloom. Before your eyes will magically play—the sweetest of days in

mid-June.

Captains

Were they poets from the start,

or did they materialize

from some high point of pleasure

in society's sweet disguise?

It's hard to be a poet, Lord.

The wallpaper in my rooms

is made of hurried rejection slips

and others swept with lonely brooms.

And yet they sit immortalized—

kings, and queens, and gods—

high, almighty, unstylized—

captains to the odd.

Applaud!

Applaud!

Applaud!

OHIO

The river moves like a song

south along the banks of

industrial towns:

Weirton,

Steubenville,

Follansbee.

It winds through Wheeling

for the jamboree,

lingers for the culture in

Cincinnati.

It doesn't discriminate—this river.

It is easily Appalachian

as it rolls around the bend

greeting folks

in Covington and beyond.

The river has a heart.

It sees a need and fills it—no

questions asked.

The law of nature is to give

what is needed, and so it does.

A river has human attributes:

a mouth,

an arm,

a leg.

It is a body of water

with arteries.

The Iroquois Indians

called it the "great river."

She is—a ruling matriarch full of life.

Our job is to care for her

all the way to the Mississippi.

Review Questions

What poems in *Oh god, Papa* appealed to you most?

Why did they appeal to you? Did they evoke a feeling, a mood? Or did you simply enjoy them for their rhythmic movement? Both?

Do you like poetry that helps you relate to your own feelings or surroundings? Did you find anything in this volume that was helpful in relating to your own circumstances?

What forms of poetry do you most appreciate and why?

After reading Freda's poems, do you think she has a handle on what it takes to write poetry effectively?

Who is your favorite poet and why? Is there one particular poem by her or him that you can recite without looking at the text?

Do you think poetry is something to be savored by everyone, or is it for the classroom and literary studies?

Appendix A

A Poetry Primer

What is Poetry?

Poetry is a word of Greek origin which means "to create." It is a form of literature that uses rhythmic and aesthetic qualities of language to communicate. Poetry was first used to record historical and cultural activities among various clans and tribes. This information, sung long before it was written down, preserved important information needed by future generations. These singing poets were known as troubadours or bards.

Modern folk singers who share stories through their songs are similar to the bards of old. One popular folk singer is Bob Dylan. Dylan has a knack for writing lyrics that stay with the listener. Lyrics are very similar to poems, but have a definite pattern that allows for a repeated chorus.

Poetry never grows old. Anything from William Shakespeare to Mary Oliver can be found on current book store shelves. Even the big screen sells poetry. Robin Williams portrayed an eccentric professor who taught the value of poetry to his students in the wildly popular 1989 film, *Dead Poets Society*. A famous line from the movie is, "carpe diem!" or seize the day, a phrase which originated with the writings of the Roman poet, Horace (65 B.C. - 8 B.C.).

Various forms of poetry evoke different moods in readers. When we think of the poetry of Robert Frost, we instantly think of the rhyming poem Stopping by the Woods on a Snowy Evening, and yet, Frost wrote more complicated and exacting verse. We remember the former poem because it is simple, picturesque, and evokes the mood of riding in that sleigh on a winter's evening. The mood varies throughout the poem. Some say the poem refers to death, and others prefer to think the poem is simply a lovely depiction of the New England countryside in winter. My favorite Frost poem is Mending Wall. It is not a rhyming poem, but it has rhythm. It is a fine example of blank verse.

Reading poetry for pure pleasure is enough reason to visit the library or bookstore for a few collections, but in addition, one can learn about other continents, cultures, and time periods through the reading of poetry. Poems are open windows on life across the ages.

A Few Forms of Poetry

Blank verse-a poem with no rhyme, but with iambic pentameter, meaning it has a set number of 5 feet per line, each foot being 2 syllables long.

Free verse-an irregular form of poetry in which the content is free of traditional rules.

Haiku-a traditional form of Japanese poetry. Haiku poems have three lines. The first and the last lines have 5 syllables. The middle line has seven syllables. The lines rarely rhyme. The haiku typically evokes images of nature.

Lyric-a poem which expresses personal feelings, typically spoken in the first person. It has a lyrical or songlike quality.

Narrative poetry-a form of poetry that tells a story, often using the voice of the narrator and characters in the poem as well.

Ode-a poem praising a person, place, or thing.

Sonnet-a poem consisting of 14 patterned lines with a particular rhyming scheme.

Poetic Devices

Alliteration-the occurrence of the same letter or sound at the beginning of closely connected words.

End Rhyme-just as it says, the rhyme occurs at the end of the line(s). The sonnet is one type of poem that uses end rhyme.

Hyperbole-exaggeration

Imagery-visually descriptive or figurative language as in a literary work.

Internal Rhyme-rhyme within the lines of poems.

Metaphor-a figure of speech that identifies something as being similar to some unrelated thing for rhetorical effect.

Onomatopoeia-the use of words that describes the sound it is trying to convey. The words *screech, meow,* and *buzz* are examples of onomatopoeia.

Personification-applying personal attributes to something that is non-personal, such as a ship having feminine qualities.

Write Your Own Poetry

Here are a few subjects for writing poems:

Animals

Challenges

Ecology/Nature

Family

Friends

Hate

Heroes/People/Characters

History

Home

Life

Love

Peace

Spirituality/Religion

War

First line sentence fragments to get you started:

No one knew

Life is a classroom

What I wouldn't give to

The rooster hid behind

Who gave you permission to

Up on a hill, secluded from view

The river wound away

That's too delicious not to

It's just your little humbug way of

Paris has the Eiffel tower, so

The knot in my throat

The ribbons in your hair

How long must I imagine

Dappled treasures in the sand

The flag was whipping

Write your own poem here:

Write your own poem here:

Further Reading

Poets & Writers Mentioned in this Book:

John Ashbery

Emily Dickinson

George Eliot

Ralph Waldo Emerson

Alan Ginsberg

Gerard Manley Hopkins

Jack Kerouac

D.H. Lawrence

C.S. Lewis

Thomas Merton

John Steinbeck

Dylan Thomas

Henry David Thoreau

Walt Whitman

William Butler Yeats

Appendix B

Acknowledgements

About the Author

Epilogue

Photo

Acknowledgements

My thanks to the following periodicals in which some of the poems in this volume first appeared, and to the editors and judges who found something to be savored along the way. Many of these poems were first published under my pen name, Noël Bleu.

"Papa"—*Midwest Poetry Review*, Best New Poet award from *MPR*

"Sugar Creek"—*Writer's Digest* international winner, critique in *WD*, and the Outstanding Ohioan award

"Marking Time"—*Writer's Digest* international winner

"Apple Towns"—*Midwest Poetry Review* first place winner

"Etude in White"—*Lyric* literary magazine

"Harmony"—*House Blessings* and *Karma Road* nonfiction books

"Things that Stay"—*Best of 1994*, Ohio Poetry Day Association, Mount Union College

"Putting by"—*Midwest Poetry Review* regional winner

"Enough"—*Quiz and Quill*, Otterbein University

"Knowing"—*Midwest Poetry Review* regional winner

Photo Credits: Color cover and matching black and white photo front insert "Freda, age 2" by Freda M. Chaney; "About the Author" photo page 117, Creative Talent Modeling Agency; "A Rare Moment with Papa" photo page 121, Anonymous.

Much gratitude to my brilliant husband, Dr. Norman Chaney, who has encouraged my love of poetry and writing for three decades.

About the Author

Freda has published several award-winning poems. Her best work is known for its crisp metaphors and sharp imagery. "Papa," the theme poem for this collection, was written in 1986. It won The Best New Poet award from *Midwest Poetry Review*. In 1994 *Writer's Digest* magazine published a critique about her winning sonnet "Sugarcreek," noting her unique styling of an otherwise traditional sonnet form. The poem won her the Outstanding Ohioan award from the Ohio House of Representatives. *Oh god, Papa*, is her first published collection of poetry. She also writes nonfiction and fiction books, short stories, magazine articles, and blogs. She studied creative writing at Otterbein University and earned her doctorate in holistic theology from AIHT. She lives with her husband, Dr. Norman Chaney, in Central Ohio.

Epilogue

"I grew up in the heartland where the strings of my soul are still plucked by the people who live on the land, love its crudeness and its cream, and set to rights what matters most at 6:00 a.m. heading out to plow."

~ Freda M. Chaney

A Rare Moment with Papa

Made in United States
Orlando, FL
16 October 2024